AMAZING
JUNIOR
ATLAS
DINOSAURS

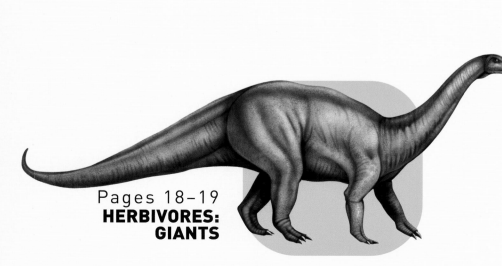

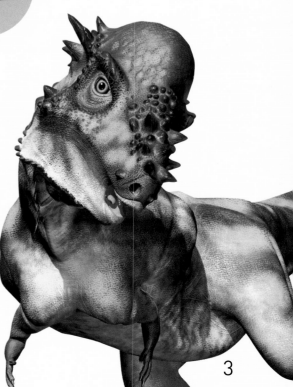

The age of dinosaurs
THE MESOZOIC ERA

THE MESOZOIC ERA

A pet dinosaur? Impossible! Dinosaurs went extinct 66 million years ago, but before that, they roamed the Earth for millions and millions of years. The period in which the dinosaurs lived is called the Mesozoic Era. It lasted more than 160 million years. That's such a long period of time that researchers have divided the period into three smaller pieces— the Triassic period, the Jurassic period, and the Cretaceous period.

THE TRIASSIC, JURASSIC, AND CRETACEOUS PERIODS

Dinosaurs lived on Earth for millions of years, but they didn't all live at the same time. Some early kinds went extinct, while new species of dinosaurs kept coming along. So the first dinosaurs were different from those living at the end of the Mesozoic Era. For instance, when the first Tyrannosaurus rex was born, the last Stegosaurus had already died 80 million years earlier.

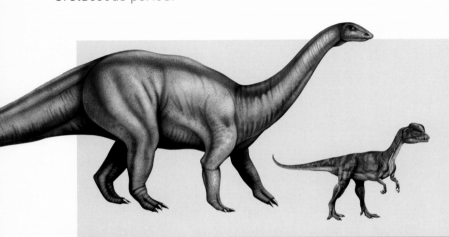

Starting 252 million years ago. **TRIASSIC**

Starting 145 million years ago. **CRETACEOUS**

BIG AND SMALL

When we say "dinosaurs," we're talking about a very diverse group of animals. They came in all shapes and sizes. Some ate meat, while others preferred plants. There were dinosaurs as big as a five-story building, but others were as small as a turkey.

TERRIBLE LIZARD

Before people had ever heard of dinosaurs, fossils had already been found. People thought that such big bones must belong to giants or dragons! Only later, in 1841, did British researcher Richard Owen realize that these big bones belonged to an animal that had become extinct. He put together the Greek words *deinos* and *sauros* and named them dinosaurs. *Deinos* means "terrible" and *sauros* is "lizard," so *dinosaur* translates to "terrible lizard." We now know that dinosaurs are not lizards at all.

Starting 201 million years ago. **JURASSIC**

DISASTER STRIKES

Why did all the dinosaurs die out 66 million years ago? And not only the dinosaurs, but most other animals died out too. It's clear that the animals encountered a worldwide disaster, but no one knows precisely what happened!

Was it caused by a volcano or a meteorite? Or did the animals just become ill?
These are questions that keep researchers occupied.

66 million years ago.

HUMANS

With the dinosaurs gone, other animals such as mammals had a chance to develop. People are mammals too. The first humans were born only 200,000 years ago. So we've been here for almost 165 million years less than the dinosaurs.

Starting 2.5 million years ago. **PLEISTOCENE**

The age of dinosaurs
WHAT DID THE WORLD LOOK LIKE?

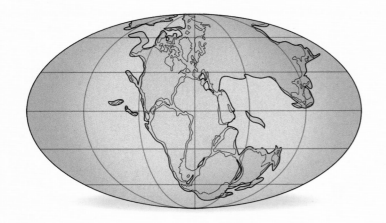

SUPERCONTINENT

When the dinosaurs walked on Earth, the planet looked very different from how it looks today. For one thing, at that time, the continents we know today did not yet exist. Instead of there being seven continents, all the land was stuck together in one big chunk, surrounded by water. This land was called Pangaea. And the dinosaurs all lived on this one "supercontinent."

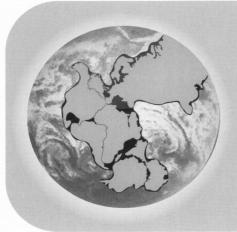

PANGAEA SPLITTING APART

Millions of years later, the supercontinent on which all the animals lived split and broke apart, scattering the dinosaurs with it. Between all these continents came seas and oceans, but dinosaurs couldn't swim. Stuck on their own land, they adapted to their new climate and environment. Eventually, different kinds of dinosaurs developed on each continent.

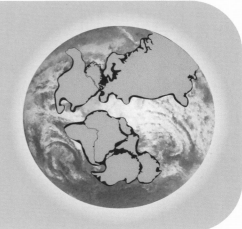

COLD-BLOODED REPTILES?

How many types of dinosaurs existed? Nobody knows! But we do know that there were a great many of them. Dinosaurs were a kind of reptile. They laid eggs, like tortoises and lizards, and some had thick, bumpy skin, like crocodiles. But unlike reptiles, some dinosaurs might have had feathers, like birds.

Reptiles are cold-blooded animals. This means that they can't warm their own bodies but need the sun to get warm. Researchers used to think that dinosaurs were cold-blooded too.
Recently, many researchers changed their minds. They now think that dinosaurs might have been warm-blooded.

LIFE BEGINS

When our planet was very young, nothing could live on it. After millions of years, the first plants and animals started to exist in the water. But Earth changed, eventually making life on land possible. Plants and trees began to cover the earth and some animals moved out of the sea to live on the land. Later, some of these animals evolved and learned to fly.

The age of dinosaurs
DINOSAUR LIFE

Mother and herd

Dinosaurs laid their eggs in nests. The mothers had to protect their nests from hungry animals who wanted to steal an egg for dinner. Many dinosaurs nested in groups. It was easier to protect their little ones in groups than alone.

The young of most carnivorous dinosaurs could take care of themselves and left the nest as soon as they hatched. Little herbivores, on the other hand, were helpless, so their moms took care of them for a long time.

The eggs

Try to imagine a dinosaur as a tiny baby! Like tortoises and birds, dinosaurs laid eggs. Dinosaur eggs came in all shapes, colors, and sizes. A giant dinosaur didn't necessarily lay giant eggs. The eggs of a long-necked dinosaur were "only" the size of a football!

Fossilized nests

A chicken sits on her eggs to keep them warm. Of course a big dinosaur couldn't do that, or they'd crush their eggs! So they covered them with plants and leaves. Some of these eggs never hatched and their fossilized remains can be found today.

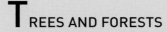

Trees and forests

Can you imagine a world without flowers or fruit? Most dinosaurs could! Flowers only started to bloom and fruits to grow toward the end of their era. Before then, herbivorous dinosaurs had to make do with hundreds of different kinds of plants and trees, such as ferns, pines, and palm trees.

Grass and plants

Most of the dinosaurs never felt grass beneath their feet or ran through a colorful, flowering meadow. Grass only started to grow at the end of the dinosaur era. Some researchers believe that when flowers started to grow, dinosaurs got hay fever from all the pollen. Those would have been some loud sneezes!

WHAT'S FOR DINNER?

What do you like to eat? Pancakes, apples, a burger maybe? Just like people, not all dinosaurs had the same food preferences.

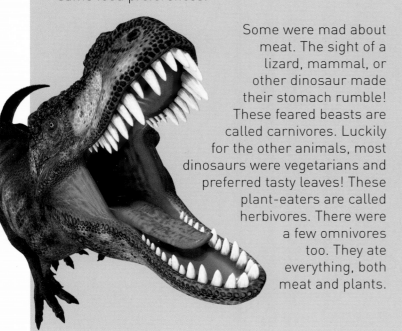

Some were mad about meat. The sight of a lizard, mammal, or other dinosaur made their stomach rumble! These feared beasts are called carnivores. Luckily for the other animals, most dinosaurs were vegetarians and preferred tasty leaves! These plant-eaters are called herbivores. There were a few omnivores too. They ate everything, both meat and plants.

HERBIVORE FEATURES

The plant-eating dinosaurs had flat teeth, good for grinding down plants and twigs for food. Some swallowed their leafy meal in one go, without chewing! Luckily, they had long intestines and a big stomach to digest all that unchewed food.

CARNIVORE FEATURES

The meat-eaters looked scary with their mouths full of big, pointy teeth that were as sharp as knives. This enabled them to bite their prey and tear it to pieces. Unlike the herbivores, their digestive systems were short.

Imagine a warm, dry, barren desert with few plants. That's the environment in which the first dinosaurs lived. After millions of years, the climate changed. It stayed warm but rained more, turning deserts into swamps. Thick forests grew, and the world became green and fresh, giving the big, plant-eating dinosaurs more than enough to eat!

Fossils
AND PALEONTOLOGISTS

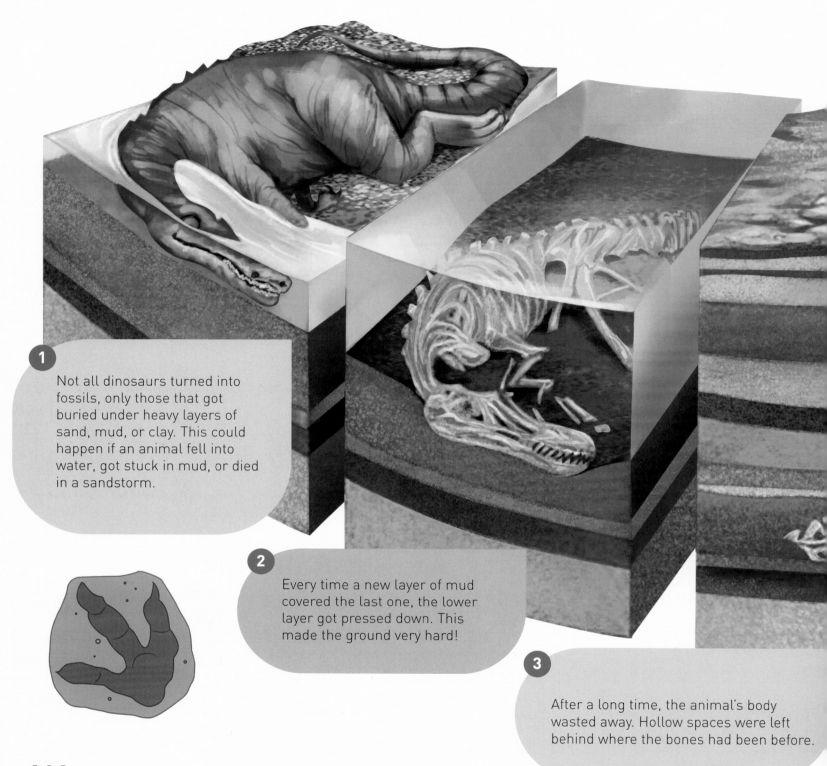

1 Not all dinosaurs turned into fossils, only those that got buried under heavy layers of sand, mud, or clay. This could happen if an animal fell into water, got stuck in mud, or died in a sandstorm.

2 Every time a new layer of mud covered the last one, the lower layer got pressed down. This made the ground very hard!

3 After a long time, the animal's body wasted away. Hollow spaces were left behind where the bones had been before.

WHAT ARE FOSSILS?

You've never met a living dinosaur, have you? When they died out 66 million years ago, they disappeared from the earth. None remained when humans existed. Although we have never seen them, we know that dinosaurs were real. This is because many remains have been found of animals and plants from the era of the dinosaurs. They're so old that they've turned to stone! We call these hardened remains *fossils*. Besides bones, other fossils can be found, such as footprints, feathers, eggs, nests, or even poop.

4

Over time, these hollow spaces filled with materials from the ground. These hardened into stone. This made copies of the actual dinosaur bones. Millions of years after its death, the dinosaur turned into a fossil.

5

Finding fossils hidden in the ground is difficult. Fortunately, erosion helps. Over time, the uppermost layers of the soil get washed away by water or blown away by the wind. Eventually, the layer containing the fossil is uncovered and the fossil can be seen at the surface.

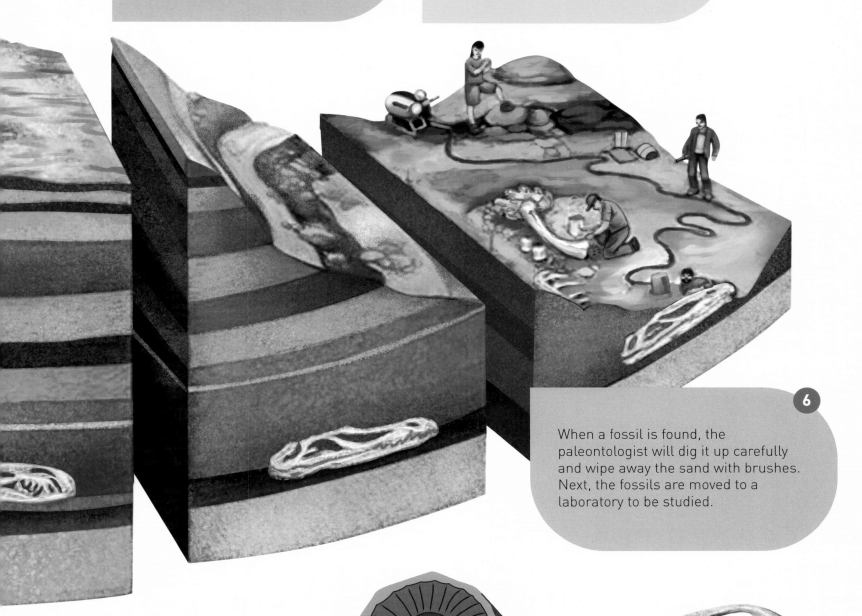

6

When a fossil is found, the paleontologist will dig it up carefully and wipe away the sand with brushes. Next, the fossils are moved to a laboratory to be studied.

Paleontologists

Paleontologists are scientists who try to understand fossils. By carefully studying these old dinosaur remains, paleontologists try to find out what a dinosaur might have looked like and how it lived.

The stone in which fossils are found can often tell scientists when the animal lived and what its habitat was like. It might even tell them about the dinosaur's behavior, its favorite food, and the way it moved. Paleontologists must be clever detectives to learn all that from a stone!

Carnivores
BIG

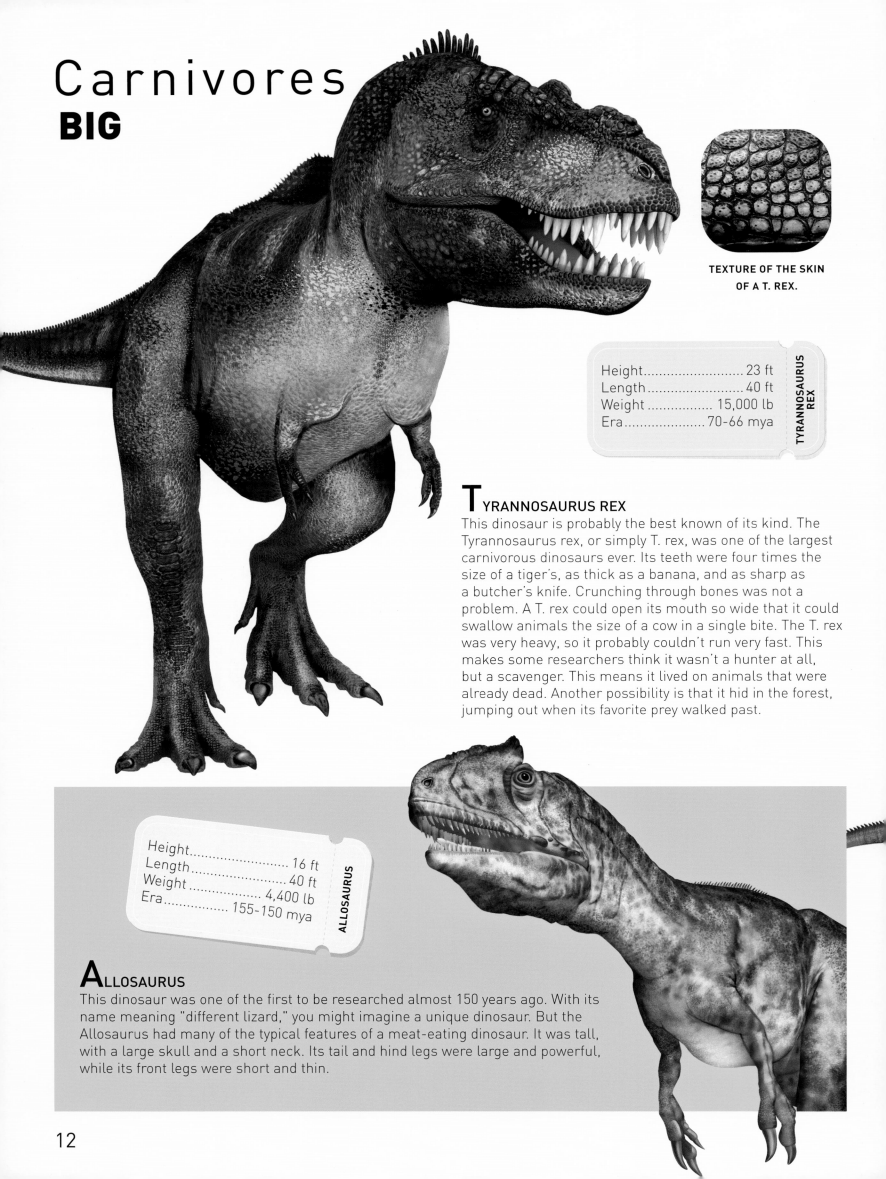

TEXTURE OF THE SKIN
OF A T. REX.

Height	23 ft	
Length	40 ft	TYRANNOSAURUS REX
Weight	15,000 lb	
Era	70-66 mya	

Tyrannosaurus rex

This dinosaur is probably the best known of its kind. The Tyrannosaurus rex, or simply T. rex, was one of the largest carnivorous dinosaurs ever. Its teeth were four times the size of a tiger's, as thick as a banana, and as sharp as a butcher's knife. Crunching through bones was not a problem. A T. rex could open its mouth so wide that it could swallow animals the size of a cow in a single bite. The T. rex was very heavy, so it probably couldn't run very fast. This makes some researchers think it wasn't a hunter at all, but a scavenger. This means it lived on animals that were already dead. Another possibility is that it hid in the forest, jumping out when its favorite prey walked past.

Height	16 ft	
Length	40 ft	ALLOSAURUS
Weight	4,400 lb	
Era	155-150 mya	

Allosaurus

This dinosaur was one of the first to be researched almost 150 years ago. With its name meaning "different lizard," you might imagine a unique dinosaur. But the Allosaurus had many of the typical features of a meat-eating dinosaur. It was tall, with a large skull and a short neck. Its tail and hind legs were large and powerful, while its front legs were short and thin.

Giganotosaurus

Not as big as the largest carnivores of its kind, such as the Spinosaurus, the Giganotosaurus was still one of the biggest meat-eating dinosaurs ever. It was probably one of the most dangerous predators around.

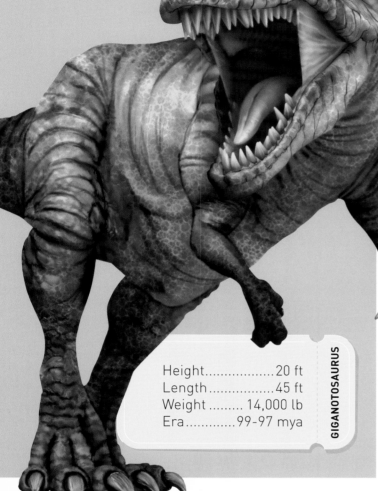

GIGANOTOSAURUS	
Height	20 ft
Length	45 ft
Weight	14,000 lb
Era	99-97 mya

ACROCANTHOSAURUS	
Height	13 ft
Length	38 ft
Weight	13,000 lb
Era	112 mya

Acrocanthosaurus

Only slightly smaller than the T. rex, this was not a carnivore to mess with. It wasn't a fast runner, but it was strong. It ate sauropods and even Ankylosaurs, which had strong, well-armored skin.
The Acrocanthosaurus had tall spines running along its neck, back, and tail, giving it a small sail.

This dinosaur probably held its head downward most of the time. How do we know? The shaft of its inner ear! So you see, even the smallest clues can help researchers to find out more about a dinosaur.

Carcharodontosaurus

Known for its long, sharp, pointy teeth, this dinosaur is named the "jagged-toothed lizard." Its teeth made it a successful hunter; it could easily rip the flesh off its prey. The Carcharodontosaurus had a long, pointy head and a big jaw. Luckily, we didn't live back then, since it would have been able to swallow an adult human in one bite!

CARCHARODONTOSAURUS	
Height	16 ft
Length	43 ft
Weight	15,000 lb
Era	100-93 mya

Carnivores
SMALL

OVIRAPTOR	
Height	4 ft
Length	6.5 ft
Weight	75 lb
Era	75 mya

Oviraptor

When researchers first found a small, unknown dinosaur near a nest full of eggs and the bones of a Protoceratops, they came to a simple conclusion: the small dinosaur must have wanted to steal the Protoceratops's eggs. So they called the unknown animal Oviraptor, which means "egg thief." Many years later another nest was found containing the same kind of eggs. On top of the nest sat a brooding Oviraptor and inside one of the eggs was an Oviraptor baby. The Oviraptor had been wrongly accused! The poor animal wasn't a thief, it was just trying to protect its nest from one!

Compsognathus

The Compsognathus was one of the smallest dinosaurs ever. This fierce, dangerous little beast was about the size of a turkey. Its favorite meal was lizards, which are fast and difficult to catch. But the Compsognathus had sharp eyes, it was small and light, and it could run very swiftly. It used its tail to avoid losing balance and falling when turning a tight corner. The poor animals caught by a Compsognathus had little chance of survival, as the dinosaur also had a mouth full of razor-sharp teeth.

COMPSOGNATHUS	
Height	16 in
Length	3 ft
Weight	7 lb
Era	150 mya

Troodon

This small, birdlike dinosaur was a fast runner and had very long, slim hind legs with retractable claws. The Troodon had large eyes set toward the front of its skull, giving it good eyesight even at night and a good depth of vision. Compared to its size, the Troodon had one of the largest brains of all the dinosaurs. But it was by no means a genius—it probably was only as smart as an ostrich today. This dinosaur might have been an omnivore, eating both animals and plants.

TROODON	
Height	3 ft
Length	8 ft
Weight	110 lb
Era	77 mya

DEINONYCHUS

The Deinonychus was a relative of the Velociraptor. Just like its cousin, it had large claws on the backs of its feet. This helped when fighting, but it may also have made it possible to climb trees.
Its tail was very stiff, which acted as a counterweight when making sharp turns.
Today, the alligator has the strongest bite of all living animals. The Deinonychus's bite was just as strong. But that was only a medium-strong bite by dinosaur standards.

Thanks to Deinonychus fossils, researchers are now sure that birds are descended from dinosaurs.

The Deinonychus may have had a feathered tail.

Height		5 ft
Length		10 ft
Weight		160 lb
Era		110 mya

DEINONYCHUS

HERRERASAURUS

The Herrerasaurus was among the first dinosaurs to walk the earth. It was named after the farmer who found it. This dinosaur had a long, narrow skull and sharp teeth. Its front legs were about half the length of its hind legs. The Herrerasaurus was a very fast hunter.

Height		3 ft
Length		10 ft
Weight		150 lb
Era		228 mya

HERRERASAURUS

Carnivores
FAST

Height......................... 20 in
Length........................ 6.5 ft
Weight .... 33 lb
Era .... 75-71 mya

VELOCIRAPTOR

VELOCIRAPTOR

Standing on four feet, the Velociraptor was about the size of a dog. With its long, strong teeth and large, sharp claws, it was a fierce carnivore. A Velociraptor didn't look for food on its own, but hunted in groups, allowing it to catch prey much bigger than itself. Its bones were hollow, making it light, so that it could run really fast on its two back feet. If all the dinosaurs were to compete in a running race, then the Velociraptor would probably be among the first to reach the finish!

Researchers have discovered that this fierce creature was probably covered with feathers!

DILOPHOSAURUS

The Dilophosaurus lived 200 million years ago. It was about 20 feet long from head to tail and rather slender. It weighed about the same as a medium-sized horse. A Dilophosaurus can be recognized by the crests that grew above each eye. This dinosaur traveled in small herds and was able to run very fast.

Height........................... 6 ft
Length........................ 20 ft
Weight .... 1,100 lb
Era........................193 mya

DILOPHOSAURUS

Herds

It's difficult for scientists to know which dinosaurs lived in herds and which lived alone. So they look for clues in fossils. When many fossils of the same kind of dinosaur are found together, this can mean that they lived together, that they were just eating near each other, or that they were fleeing from the same danger.

Fossilized footprints, however, do prove that some dinosaurs lived in great groups. In Texas a track of prints was found, left by 23 sauropods in the mud. It shows that the largest animals led the herd, followed by the younger ones. Many herbivores lived in herds, but it's difficult to say how carnivores lived, since only very few tracks of groups of meat-eating dinosaurs have been found.

Coelophysis

Its name means "hollow form," because like many other dinosaurs, this early dinosaur had hollow bones.
Did you know that dinosaurs have been to space? Well, this one has! In 1998, the US space shuttle *Endeavor* took a Coelophysis skull on a symbolic mission to outer space.

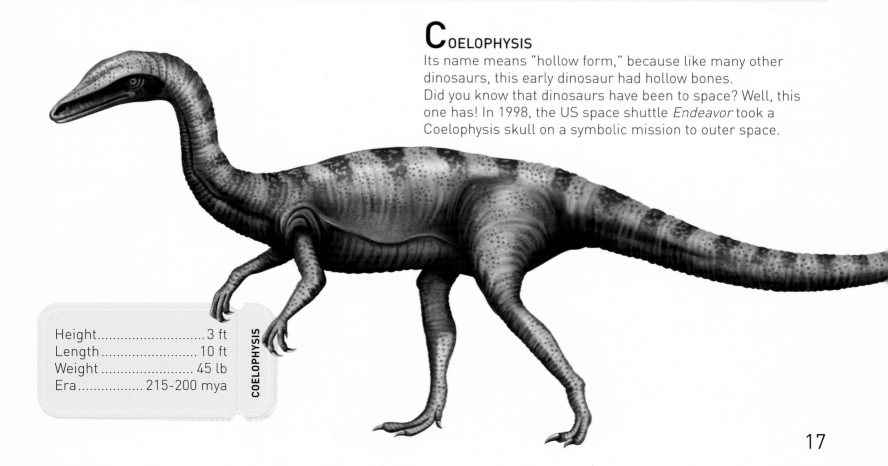

Height	3 ft
Length	10 ft
Weight	45 lb
Era	215-200 mya

COELOPHYSIS

Herbivores
GIANTS

MELANOROSAURUS	
Height	8 ft
Length	26 ft
Weight	2,900 lb
Era	227-221 mya

Melanorosaurus

This giant herbivore is one of the earliest dinosaurs and one of the first sauropods ever. Although it had a long neck, it was short compared to other, more recent sauropods. The Melanorosaurus had only eight teeth, which was typical of these early giants.

Argentinosaurus

One of the biggest dinosaurs to ever live was without a doubt the Argentinosaurus. And it was heavy too! This giant may have weighed as much as six double-decker buses! But as a baby, it started out small. A newborn Argentinosaurus weighed only around 11 pounds, not much more than a human baby.

ARGENTINOSAURUS	
Height	24.5 ft
Length	115 ft
Weight	220,000 lb
Era	94-97 mya

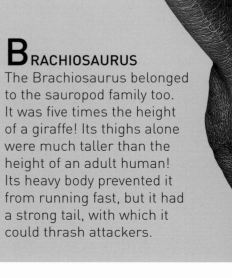

BARAPASAURUS	
Height	20 ft
Length	60 ft
Weight	106,000 lb
Era	186-170 mya

Barapasaurus

Named the "big-legged lizard," this sauropod needed to eat so much food that it didn't chew a single meal, although its teeth were about 2 inches long. It just swallowed leaves and branches whole.

Brachiosaurus

The Brachiosaurus belonged to the sauropod family too. It was five times the height of a giraffe! Its thighs alone were much taller than the height of an adult human! Its heavy body prevented it from running fast, but it had a strong tail, with which it could thrash attackers.

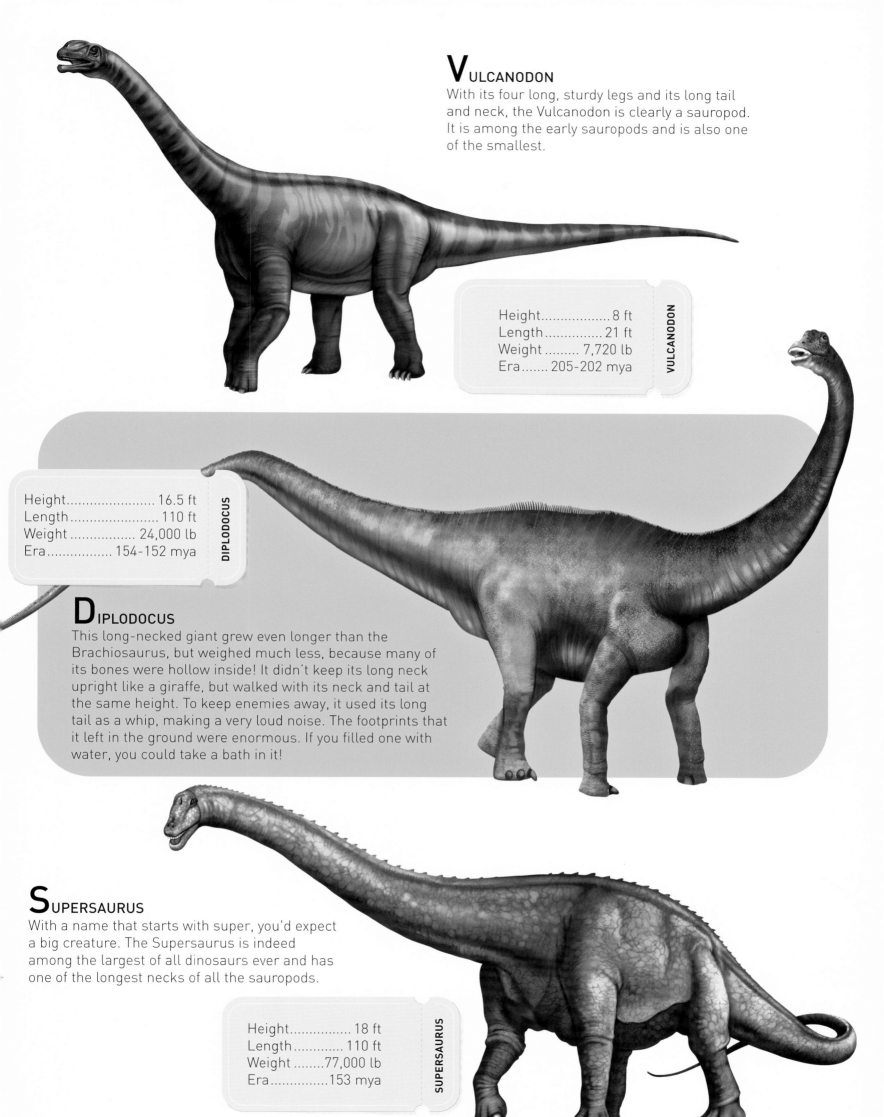

Vulcanodon

With its four long, sturdy legs and its long tail and neck, the Vulcanodon is clearly a sauropod. It is among the early sauropods and is also one of the smallest.

Height	8 ft
Length	21 ft
Weight	7,720 lb
Era	205-202 mya

VULCANODON

Height	16.5 ft
Length	110 ft
Weight	24,000 lb
Era	154-152 mya

DIPLODOCUS

Diplodocus

This long-necked giant grew even longer than the Brachiosaurus, but weighed much less, because many of its bones were hollow inside! It didn't keep its long neck upright like a giraffe, but walked with its neck and tail at the same height. To keep enemies away, it used its long tail as a whip, making a very loud noise. The footprints that it left in the ground were enormous. If you filled one with water, you could take a bath in it!

Supersaurus

With a name that starts with super, you'd expect a big creature. The Supersaurus is indeed among the largest of all dinosaurs ever and has one of the longest necks of all the sauropods.

Height	18 ft
Length	110 ft
Weight	77,000 lb
Era	153 mya

SUPERSAURUS

Herbivores
SMALL

Heterodontosaurus

This small dinosaur had a short body with a long tail to give it balance. The Heterodontosaurus had strong front limbs with five fingers, allowing it to grasp things easily. Its hind legs were long and slim, ending in four toes. It was clearly a good runner. The skin of a Heterodontosaurus was probably covered with hairlike bristles. Its small jaw was covered by a horny beak, containing two small upper teeth and four long pointy teeth.

The Heterodontosaurus was long thought to be a herbivore, but researchers now believe that it might have been an omnivore instead.

Height.............................3 ft
Length.......................5.5 ft
Weight ....22 lb
Era.................200-190 mya

HETERODONTOSAURUS

Orodromeus

The Orodromeus was a small, fast herbivore with long hind legs. Fossils of this dinosaur have been found of adults, youngsters, hatchlings, and even eggs. This has given scientists a pretty good idea of how it grew and lived. We now know that it probably ate low-growing plants and roots and that Orodomeus's hatchlings were able to feed themselves from birth.

Height ....3 ft
Length ....8 ft
Weight ....90 lb
Era.............................77 mya

ORODROMEUS

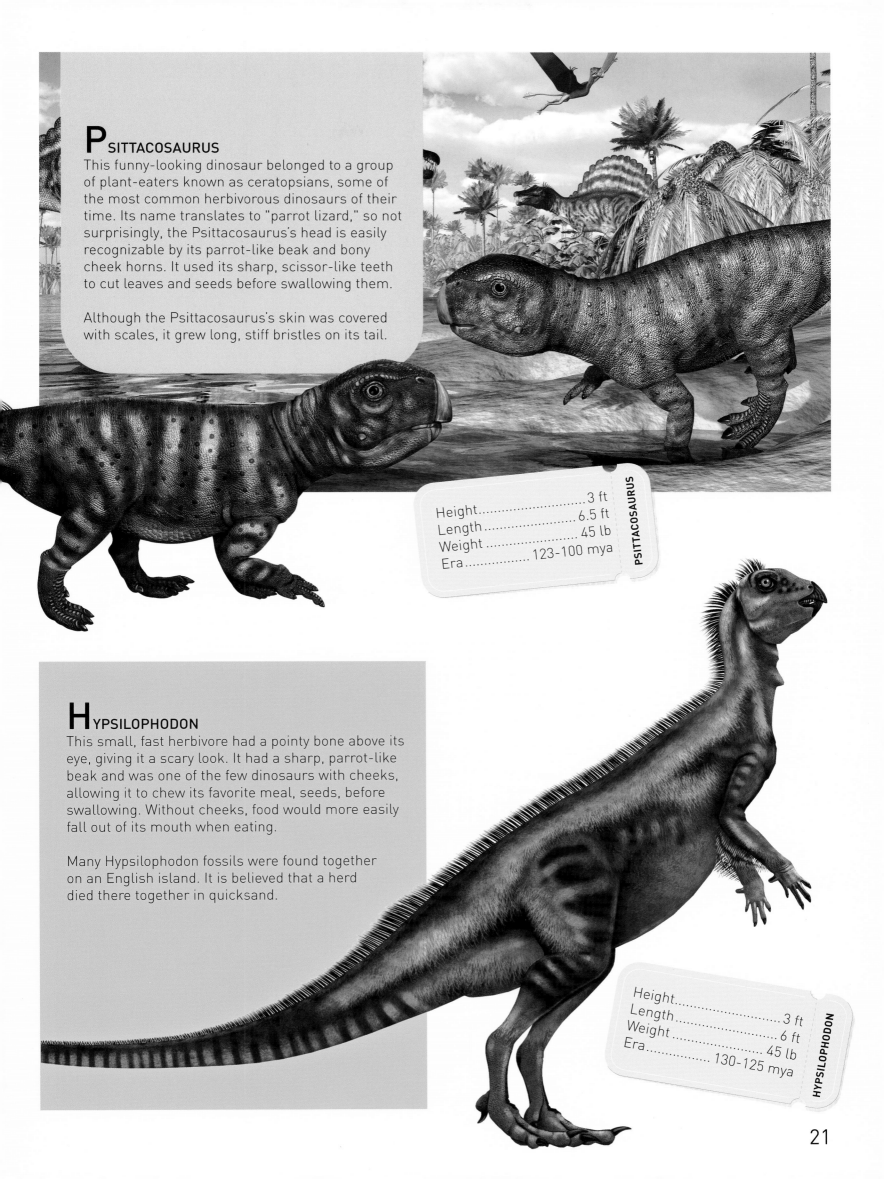

PSITTACOSAURUS

This funny-looking dinosaur belonged to a group of plant-eaters known as ceratopsians, some of the most common herbivorous dinosaurs of their time. Its name translates to "parrot lizard," so not surprisingly, the Psittacosaurus's head is easily recognizable by its parrot-like beak and bony cheek horns. It used its sharp, scissor-like teeth to cut leaves and seeds before swallowing them.

Although the Psittacosaurus's skin was covered with scales, it grew long, stiff bristles on its tail.

PSITTACOSAURUS

Height........................3 ft
Length.......................6.5 ft
Weight........................45 lb
Era.................123-100 mya

HYPSILOPHODON

This small, fast herbivore had a pointy bone above its eye, giving it a scary look. It had a sharp, parrot-like beak and was one of the few dinosaurs with cheeks, allowing it to chew its favorite meal, seeds, before swallowing. Without cheeks, food would more easily fall out of its mouth when eating.

Many Hypsilophodon fossils were found together on an English island. It is believed that a herd died there together in quicksand.

HYPSILOPHODON

Height........................3 ft
Length.......................6 ft
Weight........................45 lb
Era.................130-125 mya

21

Special
BACK

STEGOSAURUS

The Stegosaurus had seventeen big, hard, pointy plates on its back. They looked dangerous but were probably too thin to defend it against an attack by a hungry predator. Fortunately, the Stegosaurus had another powerful weapon—its tail. At the end of this were four extremely sharp spikes. These enabled it to seriously wound other animals. As soon as an enemy came too close, the Stegosaurus thrashed its tail back and forth and tried to drive the attacker away.

The plates might have helped to regulate body temperature, or maybe they just helped to attract a mate.

Fossils of other animals have been found that show just how deadly a Stegosaurus's tail could be!

Its small head and short neck only allowed the Stegosaurus to eat low-growing bushes.

The Stegosaurus only had a very small brain. It probably wasn't a very bright dinosaur.

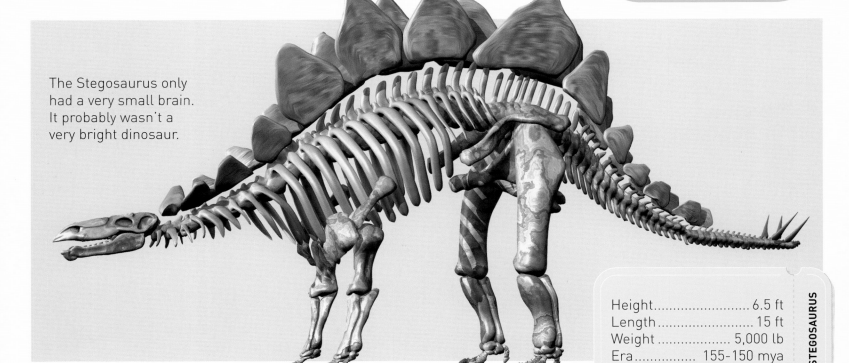

Height	6.5 ft
Length	15 ft
Weight	5,000 lb
Era	155-150 mya

STEGOSAURUS

SPINOSAURUS

A T. rex was a shorty compared to the gigantic Spinosaurus, which walked the earth 35 million years earlier. A Tyrannosaurus rex was the same height as a tower of seven grown men. To look a Spinosaurus in the eye, you might have needed nine grown men standing on each other's shoulders! Not that that would have been a great idea, as its sharp teeth made this creature extremely dangerous.

The Spinosaurus didn't only stand out for its size: its back was unusual, to say the least. The bones in its spine were extremely big and stood tall, making them look like a six-foot-high sail on the dinosaur's back. The Spinosaurus loved meat but was also one of the few dinosaurs that liked to eat fish. Its nostrils were high up on its nose, so it could easily dip its long snout into the water to catch yummy fish.

Its sail might have had the same function as the plates of a Stegosaurus.

The Spinosaurus had a long, narrow head, similar to that of a crocodile.

This dinosaur was the biggest carnivorous dinosaur ever!

Height	50 ft
Length	60 ft
Weight	33,000 lb
Era	112-97 mya

SPINOSAURUS

23

Special
WEAPONS

Styracosaurus

The Styracosaurus had an impressive head, to say the least; it looked like a Mesozoic version of today's rhinoceros.
It had a very large frill on the top of its head, with four to six horns sticking out. It also had a long horn on its nose and shorter horns growing from its cheeks.

Height	6 ft
Length	18 ft
Weight	6,600 lb
Era	75 mya

STYRACOSAURUS

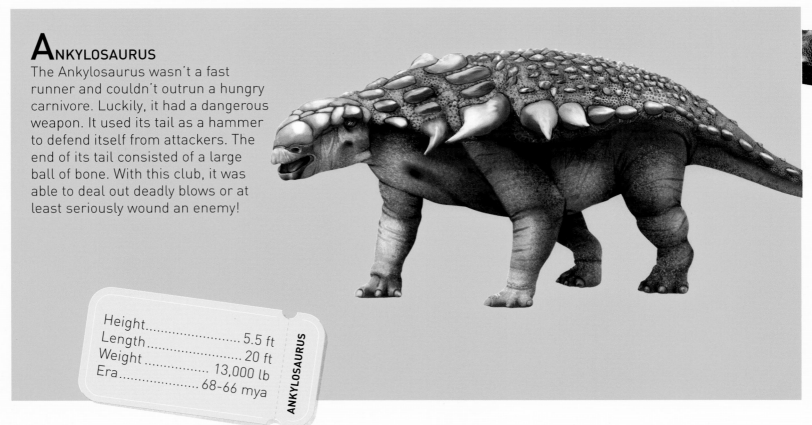

Ankylosaurus

The Ankylosaurus wasn't a fast runner and couldn't outrun a hungry carnivore. Luckily, it had a dangerous weapon. It used its tail as a hammer to defend itself from attackers. The end of its tail consisted of a large ball of bone. With this club, it was able to deal out deadly blows or at least seriously wound an enemy!

Height	5.5 ft
Length	20 ft
Weight	13,000 lb
Era	68-66 mya

ANKYLOSAURUS

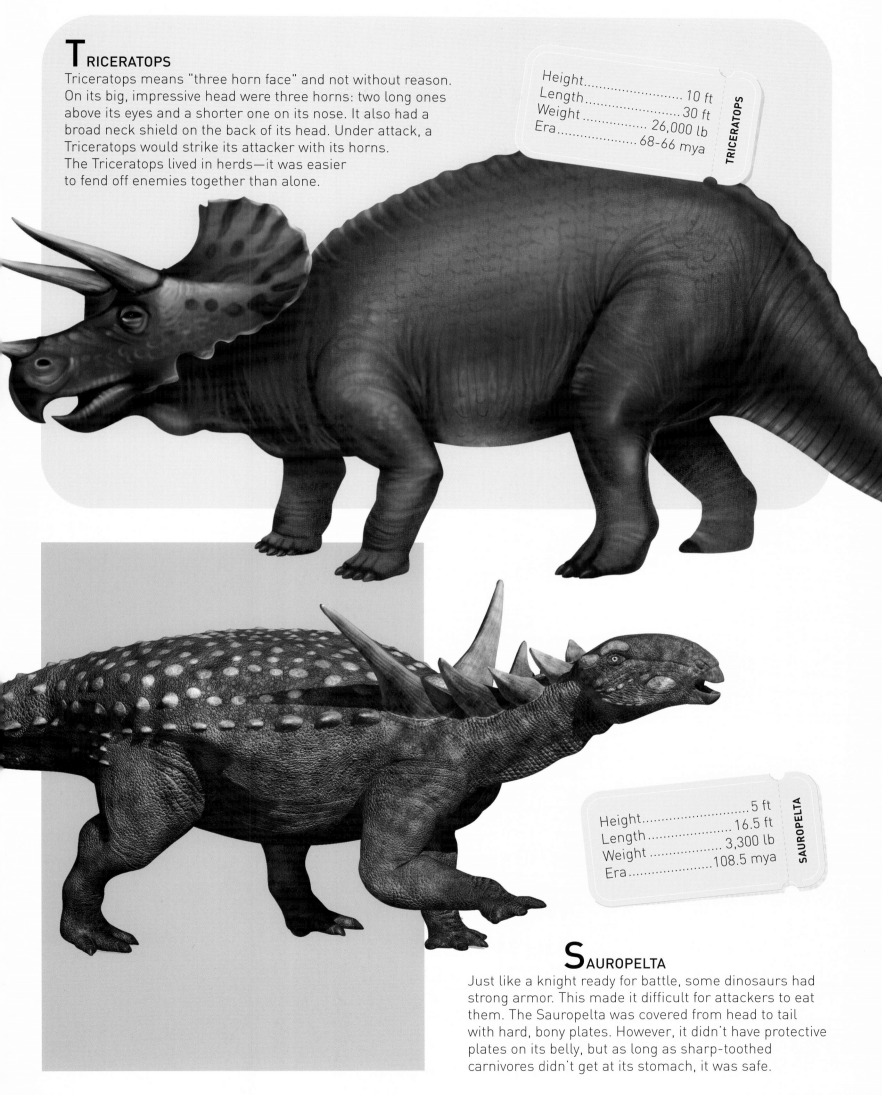

TRICERATOPS

Triceratops means "three horn face" and not without reason. On its big, impressive head were three horns: two long ones above its eyes and a shorter one on its nose. It also had a broad neck shield on the back of its head. Under attack, a Triceratops would strike its attacker with its horns. The Triceratops lived in herds—it was easier to fend off enemies together than alone.

TRICERATOPS	
Height	10 ft
Length	30 ft
Weight	26,000 lb
Era	68-66 mya

SAUROPELTA	
Height	5 ft
Length	16.5 ft
Weight	3,300 lb
Era	108.5 mya

SAUROPELTA

Just like a knight ready for battle, some dinosaurs had strong armor. This made it difficult for attackers to eat them. The Sauropelta was covered from head to tail with hard, bony plates. However, it didn't have protective plates on its belly, but as long as sharp-toothed carnivores didn't get at its stomach, it was safe.

25

Special
HEAD

It looked scary, but the Pachycephalosaurus might not have been a dangerous carnivore. Its teeth were too thin.

The bone of the "helmet" was 10 inches thick. That's about 20 times as thick as the skulls of other dinosaurs.

Pachycephalosaurus

There is no looking past it, this dinosaur had a sturdy looking head, much like a helmet! Did it use its head as a battering ram? The bone is very thick, so it might have been strong enough to survive such hard blows, but researchers can't know for sure. Many think it rammed its head into its enemies sideways. Giraffes do the same today, with much less protective headgear.

Height	4.5 ft
Length	15 ft
Weight	1,000 lb
Era	70-66 mya

PACHYCEPHALO-
SAURUS

Its short arms prove that it walked on its two hind legs.

It walked on its two long, strong hind legs.

Not only is its dome-like helmet unique, but the Pachycephalosaurus also had many bone knobs or spikes on its head and snout. Like many dinosaur features, we don't know what they were for, but they were probably for protection or decoration.

Dilophosaurus

The name Dilophosaurus means "two-crested lizard." This dinosaur indeed had crests growing above each eye. Paleontologists don't yet know why this dinosaur had these plates on its head. Was it to look scarier? Or perhaps it helped them to smell prey? Many scientists actually believe that this was just a way of attracting a mate. It is still a mystery that we might never be able to solve.

Parasaurolophus

The Parasaurolophus had a very distinctive feature—a sort of trumpet on its head! This was a three-foot-long hollow tube of hard, bony material, with which it could make a tooting noise. Researchers think it used this trumpet to warn other Parasaurolophuses about danger, so that they could find safety. These dinosaurs lived in big groups. Imagine the noise that they must have made when they all used their trumpets at the same time!

27

Air
PTEROSAURS

PTEROSAUR

Pterosaur means "winged lizard," so it comes as no surprise that this prehistoric reptile could fly. Technically, pterosaurs weren't dinosaurs, but they were related. They did live and die out in the same period as the dinosaurs. There were lots of different kinds of pterosaurs. Many had long tails. Their bodies were covered with little hairs and their big wings were covered with feathers or skin, like a bat's wings.

DIMORPHODON

The Dimorphodon was about the size of a big goose, but with its wings outstretched, it was as broad as a 9-year-old child is tall! It also had long legs, a short neck, and a long tail. But the most noticeable thing was its big, round head, which was longer than its body!

Just as you have sharp incisors at the front and flat molars at the back of your mouth, the Dimorphodon had two different kinds of teeth. The front of its beak was filled with long teeth, good for fishing. With the smaller teeth at the back of its jaw, it chewed its freshly caught fish into small pieces.

QUETZALCOATLUS

Can you imagine a giraffe soaring through the sky? The biggest and heaviest pterosaur discovered so far is Quetzalcoatlus. Its body was as big as a giraffe's. With its enormous wings, it was the biggest flying creature ever. Flying through the sky, it could cover great distances, like a glider! But on land, it used its four legs to walk.

PTERANODON

The Pteranodon had a large crest at the back of its head and a long beak, but no teeth. Its name actually means "wing without tooth." Much like a pelican, it used its bill to scoop fish out of the water and swallowed them whole. No teeth needed for that! It also had very broad wings—20 feet wide when spread out. That's almost two cars, one behind the other. But its body was small. The Pteranodon was not much bigger than a turkey!

Length	8 ft
Wingspan	20 ft
Weight	200 lb
Era	125-120 mya

PTERANODON

BAMBIRAPTOR

Imagine walking in the park and stumbling over a dinosaur. That's how a 14-year-old boy discovered a complete Bambiraptor skeleton.

This birdlike raptor is not a pterosaur but a dinosaur. It was covered in feathers and its bones showed many similarities to modern birds. But it couldn't fly—its arms were too short. Despite its cute name, this raptor was an excellent hunter, and it had opposable fingers, or thumbs, on its front claws, which made it possible to grab things easily.

Length	3 ft
Wingspan	3 ft
Weight	11 lb
Era	75 mya

BAMBIRAPTOR

29

Water

Length..................46 ft
Weight.................4,400 lb
Era......................80.5 mya

Monsters at sea

The dinosaurs may have ruled the land, but the sea belonged to gigantic, carnivorous reptiles. Some of them had ancestors who had lived as land animals first. When there was more food for them in the sea, they moved there. Their bodies adapted to life in the water and their feet became webbed or they grew flippers. Most marine reptiles spent most of the time swimming in the water, but there were some that also crawled around on the seabed, looking for food. There was one tiny problem, however: these marine reptiles couldn't breathe underwater! Luckily, they had a good solution—after each dive, they stuck their heads out of the water for a gulp of air!

The teeth in its small head were incredibly sharp and dangerous. They stuck out a little, to grip fish better.

Elasmosaurus

The plesiosaurs had long necks, some longer than others. The Elasmosaurus had the longest neck of all—it was longer than its body and tail put together! Its neck even weighed so much that the animal couldn't raise its head far above the water.

Other sea creatures had to watch out for these water monsters. If an Elasmosaurus attacked from above, then prey would be warned by the giant shadow that it cast. So this giant hunted fish by swimming underneath them. As unlucky fish swam overhead, the Elasmosaurus would snap its neck upward with a lightning-quick movement and gobble up its meal!

A scientist once made the mistake of putting an Elasmosaurus's head onto its tail instead of its neck.

The Elasmosaurus had a rather slim body and four paddle-shaped flippers.

Due to its weight, the Elasmosaurus was a slow swimmer.

PLESIOSAURUS

In addition to the long-necked dinosaurs on land, there were also reptiles with long necks in the water. These swimming reptiles were the plesiosaurs. They were carnivores. One of the plesiosaurs was Plesiosaurus. It hunted fish and marine animals. Its four flippers looked a bit like big paddles, but this animal didn't row. It moved its flippers back and forth, like a penguin, "flying" through the water!

Unlike the dinosaurs and most reptiles, the plesiosaurs didn't hatch out of eggs. Their babies were born in the water and could swim right away.

Length .... 11.5 ft
Weight .... 1,100 lb
Era .... 199-175 mya

PLESIOSAURUS

LIOPLEURODON

The Liopleurodon was a gigantic sea predator, one of the biggest and heaviest reptiles ever to have lived in the sea. It had a crocodile-like head and its mouth, full of sharp teeth, was six and a half feet long. That's longer than a tall grown-up human. It had four flippers, which enabled it to move through the water extremely quickly.

Like a real sea "monster," the Liopleurodon ate everything that it came across. Big or small, dangerous or not—it didn't matter to a Liopleurodon. With its sharp teeth, it could take on any animal. It even snapped at low-flying pterosaurs.

Length .... 26 ft
Weight .... 3,700 lb
Era................. 162-150 mya

LIOPLEURODON

31

Other
ANIMALS

Archaeopteryx

The flying reptiles shared their airspace with many insects, and after a while they were joined by a new kind of animal... birds! You wouldn't think it, but even the smallest sparrows, magpies, and blackbirds are descended from dangerous, carnivorous dinosaurs! The Archaeopteryx was one of the very first birds. It looked rather like a reptile and a bird put together. Often referred to as Urvogel or "original bird," it had no big beak, but it did have a mouth full of teeth. It also had feathers, wings, and a long tail.

Sea star

If you had been able to swim in the sea a hundred million years ago, you might have seen a sea star. Known as starfish, these star-shaped animals aren't fish at all. They've been around for a very long time. They existed long before the first dinosaurs arrived. Some types of sea star even survived more than one great extinction, like the one that killed off all the dinosaurs.

Juramaia

This small mouse-like mammal lived some 160 million years ago. Its fossils helped scientists to research the evolution of placental mammals. Unlike reptiles and birds, which lay eggs, placental mammals carry their babies inside their tummies. Humans are also placental mammals. The fossil of Juramaia proved that such mammals existed 35 million years earlier than scientists previously thought.

Because this was such an important discovery, this little animal was given a name that means "Jurassic mother."

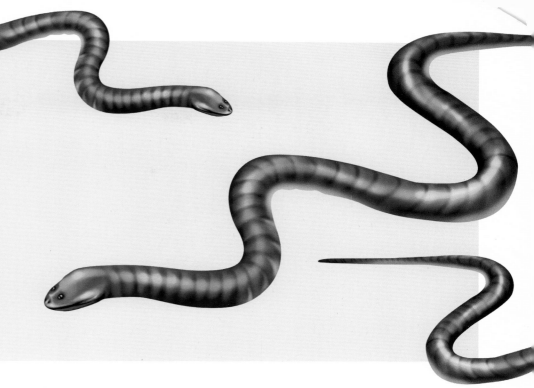

Snakes

Surely giant dinosaurs didn't fear snakes? Maybe not, but they probably kept an eye out for them! Fossils have been found of snakes that lived over 150 million years ago, so it is probable that they did sneak into dinosaur nests to steal an egg or a newborn dinosaur for dinner.

The end of the dinosaurs wasn't the end of giant reptiles. The Titanoboa lived 60 million years ago—that's 6 million years after the extinction of the dinosaurs. It was the largest and longest snake ever to slither on Earth. At almost 42 feet long, it was longer than a bus and it weighed more than a large, heavy cow.

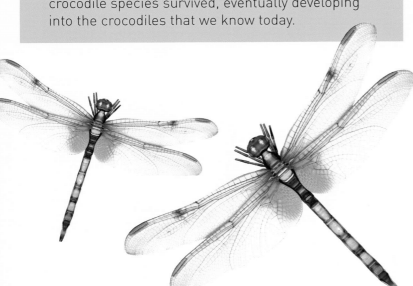

Sarcosuchus

Sarcosuchus, a crocodile-like reptile that lived alongside the dinosaurs, grew to 40 feet long. This giant must have had a huge appetite, eating everything that it could sink its teeth into, even dinosaurs! It died out with the dinosaurs, but other crocodile species survived, eventually developing into the crocodiles that we know today.

Fish

Fish have been around for over 500 million years. That's long before the first dinosaur walked on land, or the first plesiosaurs splashed around in the ocean. There were also giant fish in the time of the dinosaurs. Leedsichthys, for example, were 40 to 65 feet long. And they had teeth!

Dragonfly

Imagine you're in the park. Suddenly, a dragonfly as big as a crow flies over your head. You're startled and duck down, just to see that you've almost stepped on a centipede—and not just any centipede. This one is as long as a four-year-old child is tall! This is what insects were like in the time of the dinosaurs. Most insects then looked much like the insects we know now. They were only several sizes bigger.

The end
OF THE DINOSAURS

Worldwide disaster

Dinosaurs ruled the land for 165 million years. But 66 million years ago, something terrible happened—a worldwide disaster. In a very short period of time all the dinosaurs died out! Not only were the dinosaurs gone, but flying reptiles (such as pterosaurs), marine reptiles (such as plesiosaurs), and many other kinds of animals died out too. In total, about three out of four animals in the world went extinct.

It's clear that the animals encountered a worldwide disaster, but no one knows precisely what happened.

Meteorite

A meteorite is the most probable reason why the dinosaurs disappeared. About 66 million years ago, a piece of rock of almost six miles thick crashed down out of space and hit Earth at an enormous speed. The space rock, also called a meteorite, landed in Mexico and made a big hole in the ground of 112 miles wide!

The crash caused a big cloud of dust, preventing any sunlight from getting through. Suddenly, it went dark on Earth, and it stayed that way for a long time! Plants can't grow in the dark, so soon there was no food left for the herbivorous dinosaurs. The poor animals starved. After the carnivores had eaten the last herbivores, there was no food left for them either. That probably meant the end for all the dinosaurs.

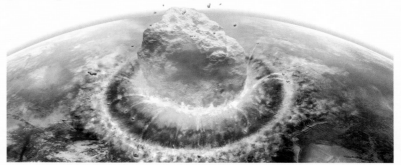

Volcanoes

Many researchers are not convinced that a meteorite was solely to blame, and point the finger at volcanoes. Toward the end of the dinosaur era, there were many enormous active volcanoes around what is currently known as India. Several volcanoes erupted extremely violently, letting off so much ash, lava, and gas that a gigantic ash cloud formed, blocking out the sunlight. Like a meteorite impact, this would have made the earth a dark, cold place. The change in climate could easily have caused the dinosaurs to die out.

ILLNESS

Some researchers are convinced that a dangerous infectious disease could have infected all the dinosaurs and many other reptiles. This might have caused them to get ill and die.

MAMMALS

Other animals, such as mammals, existed at the time of the dinosaurs. Some researchers think that mammals might have caused the dinosaurs to become extinct. Mammals were much smaller than dinosaurs, and they might have eaten the dinosaurs' eggs, so that no more young were born, and the dinosaurs died out. This theory isn't very popular among scientists.

BEFORE THE DINOSAURS

It wasn't the first time that so many animals disappeared from the earth at the same time. The same thing happened in the period just before the time of the dinosaurs.
Scientists don't know what caused that great extinction either, but it did give the dinosaurs a chance to evolve.

LIFE WENT ON

The earth must have been very quiet and empty after the disappearance of so many animals! Fortunately, there were also animals that survived the disaster. These were smaller animals that ate seeds or insects. They didn't need many plants to live. Animals that could hibernate and didn't need much food for a while also had a good chance, as did all the other animals that could easily adapt to the new situation.

Few animals survived the end of the Mesozoic era. But with the dinosaurs gone, the remaining animals were able to develop. These animals were insects, frogs, snakes, lizards, tortoises and turtles, birds, and mammals. The mammals evolved into a very diverse group of animals. And people are mammals too. So if the dinosaurs had still lived today, people would probably never have been born. Imagine that!

Giganotosaurus

Allosaurus

Tyrannosaurus rex

Acrocanthosaurus

Carcharodontosaurus

Coelophysis

Dilophosaurus

Velociraptor

Troodon

Compsognathus

Oviraptor

Herrerasaurus

Deinonychus

Barapasaurus

Diplodocus

Supersaurus

Vulcanodon

Argentinosaurus

Melanorosaurus

Brachiosaurus

Psittacosaurus

Heterodontosaurus

Hypsilophodon

Orodromeus

Stegosaurus

Spinosaurus

Ankylosaurus

Triceratops

Sauropelta

Styracosaurus

Dilophosaurus

Parasaurolophus

Pachycephalosaurus

Pteranodon

Dimorphodon

Microraptor*

Bambiraptor*

Quetzalcoatlus

Elasmosaurus

Plesiosaurus

Liopleurodon

Dragonfly

Sea star

Juramaia

Archaeopteryx

Snake

Sarcosuchus

* also dinosaurs

Sizing up
DINOSAURS

TYRANNOSAURUS REX

PARASAUROLOPHUS

DIPLODOCUS

BAMBIRAPTOR

COMPSOGNATHUS

STYRACOSAURUS